"GOOGLE SOMETHING EVERY DAY"

UNLOCKING THE POWER OF CONTINUOUS LEARNING AT ANY AGE

RICHARD ERSCHIK

TABLE OF CONTENTS

PREFACE:

As I sit down to begin writing this book, I am struck by the incredible life journey that has brought me to this moment. At 79 years young, I find myself more passionate than ever about the power of continuous learning and personal growth. It is this passion, born from a lifetime of experiences and a thirst for knowledge, which has inspired me to embark on what is my seventh book writing endeavor.

"Google Something Every Day" is not just another book; it is a manifesto for lifelong learning and self-improvement. Drawing from my own experiences as an Army Vietnam War Veteran and creator of the acclaimed MasterCourse "How to Speak and Present to a Group," I have witnessed firsthand the transformative power of removing their blinders and leading others down their own path of self-discovery. Inspired by the timeless wisdom of Admiral William H. McRaven's book, "Make Your Bed," I have come to believe that the little things we learn and do every day can have a profound impact on our mental health and overall well-being.

In this book, I aim to explore the theory of "Never Stop Learning at Any Age" and share with you how it can be applied to improve your life through the simple yet powerful act of Googling something every day.

By combining the principles of making your bed, and continuous learning, I believe you can unlock untapped potential in yourself and create positive change in your life and the world around you.

As you journey through the pages of this book, I encourage you to approach each day with a sense of curiosity and wonder. Embrace the opportunity to learn something new, no matter how small, and see where it leads you. Whether you are a seasoned computer using veteran or just beginning your quest for knowledge, remember that it's never too late to start learning.

Let's embark on this journey together, armed with the knowledge that by making our beds and Googling something every day, we can mitigate boredom and create a brighter, more fulfilling future for ourselves and those around us.

Richard Erschik

PRELUDE

Keeping mentally active has many proven benefits.

Here are 10 mental health benefits of keeping your mind active by searching on Google for information, education, and entertaining things:

1. Cognitive Stimulation: Engaging in Google searches requires mental effort, stimulating cognitive functions such as attention, memory, and problem-solving skills.

2. Continuous Learning: Actively seeking out new information on Google fosters a sense of curiosity and intellectual growth, promoting lifelong learning and personal development.

3. Distraction and Relaxation: Exploring entertaining content on Google can serve as a distraction from stressors, promoting relaxation and reducing anxiety or depressive symptoms.

4. Increased Knowledge and Awareness: Learning new information through Google searches broadens one's perspective, increases awareness of the world, and enhances feelings of competence and self-confidence.

5. Social Connection: Sharing interesting findings from Google searches with others fosters social connection and

engagement, strengthening relationships and promoting a sense of belonging.

6.   Sense of Empowerment: Access to a wealth of information empowers individuals to take control of their learning and personal growth, promoting feelings of autonomy and resilience.

7.   Mood Enhancement: Discovering entertaining or uplifting content on Google can improve mood and provide a sense of enjoyment and fulfillment.

8.   Brain Health: Keeping the mind active through Google searches may contribute to brain health and lower the risk of cognitive decline and dementia later in life.

9.   Creativity Boost: Exposing oneself to diverse information and perspectives on Google can spark creativity and inspire new ideas and insights.

10.   Problem-Solving Skills: Engaging in Google searches to find solutions to problems or answer questions hones problem-solving skills and fosters a sense of accomplishment and mastery.

These above benefits highlight the positive impact that actively engaging with information and entertainment on Google can have on your mental well-being. Now it's up to you.

INTRODUCTION:

"Google Something Every Day" is a transformative guide written by Richard Erschik, an Army Vietnam War Veteran of the mid 1960's and creator of the acclaimed self-esteem boosting and personal improvement MasterCourse, "How to Speak and Present to a Group."

Inspired by the timeless wisdom of Admiral William H. McRaven's "Make Your Bed" as one of the little things you can do every day to change your life, this book explores the theory of continuous learning at any age to improve your life. Combing these two powerful concepts it could best be said that to benefit from both practices you should first make your bed, then Google something every day.

NOTE: Before we begin this journey, together, let's address the elephant in the room and answer the question about "How" to use Google on various personal devices. Follow the instructions below to help get you on your way.

Smartphone (iOS/Android):

1. Unlock your smartphone and navigate to the home screen.

2. Locate the Google app icon, which typically looks like a colored 'G' on a white background. If you don't have the Google app installed, you can download it from the Google Play Store (Android) or the App Store (iOS).

3. Tap on the Google app icon to open it.

4. Once the app is open, you'll see a search bar at the top of the screen. Tap on the search bar to activate it.

5. Using the on-screen keyboard, type in the keywords or phrase you want to search for.

6. As you type, Google will suggest search terms based on what you've entered. You can either select one of the suggested terms or continue typing your query.

7. Once you've entered your search query, tap the "Search" button on the keyboard or press "Enter" on the keyboard to perform the search.

8. Google will display a list of search results based on your query. You can scroll through the results to find the information you're looking for.

9. Tap on any search result to view more details or visit the website associated with that result.

Tablet iOS/Android):

Using Google on a tablet is similar to using it on a smartphone. Follow the same steps outlined above for smartphones to access Google and perform a search.

PC – Personal Computer (Windows/Mac):

1. Open your web browser (e.g., Google Chrome, Mozilla Firefox, Safari, Microsoft Edge) on your PC.

2. In the address bar at the top of the browser window, type in www.google.com and press "Enter" on your keyboard to navigate to the Google homepage.

3. Once on the Google homepage, you'll see a search bar in the center of the screen.

4. Click inside the search bar to activate it.

5. Using your keyboard, type in the keywords or phrase you want to search for.

6. As you type, Google will suggest search terms based on what you've entered. You can either select one of the suggested terms or continue typing your query.

7. Once you've entered your search query, press "Enter" on your keyboard or click the "Google Search" button (usually a magnifying glass icon) to perform the search.

8. Google will display a list of search results based on your query. You can scroll through the results to find the information you're looking for.

9. Click on any search result to view more details or visit the website associated with that result.

MAC: (iMAC, MacBook Pro)

Using Google on a Mac is remarkably similar to using it on a PC. Follow the instructions above for PCs to access Google and perform a search.

That's it! You're now equipped to use Google on your smartphone, tablet, PC, or Mac to search for information and explore the world wide web.

NOTE: If you find yourself still staring at your smartphone, tablet, PC, or MAC with a look of utter confusion, fear not! Just when you think technology has outsmarted you, there's always a trusty lifeline to call upon: the younger generation. Yes, those digital wizards known as nieces, nephews, sons, daughters, grandkids, or any tech-savvy young whippersnapper will come to your rescue faster than you can say "Google it." With a flick of their fingers and a tap-tap here and there, they'll have you navigating the digital world like a pro in no time. By asking a youngster to show you how it's done, who knows, you might even learn a thing or two about emojis and TikTok dances along the way. Keep an open mind that is soon to be blown!

So Why Should You Consider Learning How to Use the likes of Google at a Late Age?

In the digital age, Google has become synonymous with information retrieval. From mundane queries to complex research endeavors,

Google is the go-to tool for worldwide use.

Astonishingly, one billion people search Google every day because beyond its surface utility lies a vast landscape of information and possibilities, waiting to be explored. Google can not only help you reference events from your life but also serve as a gateway to endless educational and entertainment opportunities.

Below Are 20 Examples of What Awaits You as Informational/ Educational And Entertainment Opportunities That Are Available To You By Googleing – For FREE:

Educational/Informational Opportunities:

1. **Google Scholar:** Access to scholarly articles and research papers across various disciplines.

2. **Google Books:** Digitized collection of books and publications, including literary classics and academic texts.

3. **Google Classroom:** Online platform for educators to create, distribute, and grade assignments.

4. **Google Arts & Culture:** Virtual tours of museums, historical landmarks, and cultural artifacts.

5. **Google Earth:** Interactive 3D mapping tool for exploring the globe and its geographical features.

6. **Google Drive:** Cloud storage service for storing and sharing documents, presentations, and other files.

7. **Google Translate:** Language translation tool for translating text, websites, and spoken words.

8. **Google Code-in:** Contest for pre-university students to contribute to open-source projects and gain real-world coding experience.

9. **Google Science Fair:** Online competition for young scientists to highlight their research projects and innovations.

10. **Google News:** Aggregated news platform providing access to a wide range of sources and perspectives.

Entertainment Opportunities:

1. **YouTube:** Video-sharing platform for watching and sharing user-generated content, including music videos, vlogs, and tutorials.

2. **Google Play Movies & TV:** Online store for renting or purchasing movies and TV shows for streaming.

3. **Google Stadia:** Cloud gaming service for playing video games without the need for dedicated gaming hardware.

4. **Google Doodles:** Interactive and animated variations of the Google logo celebrating holidays, anniversaries, and notable events.

5. **Google Arts & Culture:** Online platform for exploring artworks, cultural exhibits, and historical artifacts.

6. **Google Podcasts:** Platform for discovering and listening to podcasts on various topics and genres.

7. **Google Play Books:** Digital bookstore offering a wide selection of e-books for purchase and download.

8. **Google Maps:** Navigation tool for exploring cities, finding directions, and discovering local businesses and attractions.

9. **Google Photos:** Cloud storage service for storing, organizing, and sharing photos and videos.

10. **Google Assistant:** Virtual assistant for performing tasks, answering questions, and controlling smart devices.

The above examples highlight just a fraction of the educational and entertainment opportunities available by searching Google, highlighting the platform's versatility and impact on users' lives.

A little history: Google's journey from a humble search engine to an omnipresent force in our lives is a testament to its unparalleled effectiveness. Founded in 1998 by Larry Page and Sergey Brin, Google has evolved into a multifaceted conglomerate, offering a wide array of services, from email and cloud storage to mapping and artificial intelligence. Its ubiquity in modern society is undeniable, with billions of searches conducted daily across its various platforms. Yet, despite its omnipresence, many users only scratch the surface of Google's capabilities, unaware of the wealth of knowledge and entertainment that lies just beneath the surface.

Imagine a scenario: You're reminiscing about a childhood vacation but can't recall the exact year or location. Enter Google. By typing in a few keywords related to your trip, you can uncover a treasure trove of information, from travel blogs to archived photographs. Suddenly, the memories come flooding back, vivid and detailed, all thanks to a quick search query. Google's indexing prowess spans decades, making it a powerful tool for nostalgia seekers and history buffs alike.

But Google's utility extends beyond mere nostalgia. It serves as a digital diary of sorts, documenting the milestones and minutiae of our lives with unparalleled precision. From tracking down old classmates to revisiting past accomplishments, Google enables us to reflect on our personal journeys and celebrate the moments that shape us. Whether you're looking for the name of a long-forgotten childhood friend or the date of your high school graduation, Google is there to provide the answers, acting as a custodian of our collective memories.

However, Google's usefulness transcends individual recollection. It is a veritable treasure trove of knowledge, offering access to an incomprehensible amount of information on virtually any topic imaginable. Whether you're a student conducting research for a term paper or a professional seeking to expand your expertise, Google's search algorithms can sift through mountains of data to deliver relevant and reliable information in an instant. With each search, you embark on a journey of discovery, uncovering new insights and perspectives that enrich your understanding of the world.

Moreover, Google isn't just a passive repository of information; it actively facilitates learning through its suite of educational tools and resources. For example, Google Scholar provides access to scholarly articles and research papers across a wide range of disciplines, empowering students, and academics to stay abreast of the latest developments in their fields. Similarly, Google Books offers a vast collection of digitized books and publications, allowing readers to explore literary classics and academic texts from the comfort of their own homes. Whether you're delving into academic journals or exploring virtual museum exhibits, Google empowers individuals to pursue knowledge and expand their horizons in ways previously unimaginable. In essence, Google is not just a search engine; it's a gateway to a world of learning and enlightenment.

In addition to its educational benefits, Google also serves as a gateway to entertainment in all its forms. From streaming services like YouTube and Google Play Movies to online games and virtual reality experiences, Google offers a plethora of diversions to suit every taste and interest. Whether you're in the mood for a thought-provoking documentary or a mindless game to unwind, Google has you covered. Its recommendations algorithm ensures that you're always one click away from your next favorite movie, book, or game, keeping boredom at bay and sparking joy in the mundane.

Furthermore, Google's entertainment offerings extend beyond traditional media consumption to include interactive experiences and creative outlets. For instance, Google Arts & Culture allows users to explore the world's cultural treasures through virtual tours of museums and historical landmarks, providing a window into the past and present of humanity's artistic heritage. Similarly, Google Earth enables users to traverse the globe from the comfort of their own homes, offering stunning views of natural wonders and urban landscapes alike. Whether you're a budding artist or a seasoned performer, Google provides a platform for you to share your talents with the world and connect with like-minded individuals from across the globe. In this way, Google transcends its role as a mere search engine, evolving into a vibrant ecosystem of creativity and discovery.

Learning how to harness the power of Google is akin to unlocking a portal to infinite knowledge and entertainment. By mastering its search capabilities, you gain the ability to reference events from your past, enrich your education, and indulge in endless hours of entertainment. So, the next time you find yourself pondering a long-forgotten memory or seeking to expand your horizons, remember: Google is not just a search engine; it's a gateway to a world of possibilities. Whether you're exploring the depths of human history or embarking on a journey of self-discovery, Google is there to guide you every step of the way, opening doors to new experiences and opportunities that transcend the boundaries of space and time.

Now that I may have peaked your interest about Google in general, here are some more facts. Or you may just want to skip ahead and begin your hands-on learning ahead in Chapter 1.

1. **Origin of the Name:** Understanding the playful origin of the name "Google" highlights the founders' creative approach to tackling the challenge of organizing vast amounts of information on the internet.

2. **Stanford University Roots:** Google's origins at Stanford University underscore the significance of academic collaboration and innovation in the tech industry, shaping its early development and culture.

3. **First Google Doodle:** The creation of the first Google Doodle demonstrates the company's whimsical and unconventional approach to its brand, setting a precedent for creative and memorable interactions with users.

4. **Gmail's April Fools' Joke:** Gmail's launch as an April Fools' joke turned legitimate service showcases Google's ability to disrupt established industries with innovative products and challenge assumptions about what's possible.

5. **I'm Feeling Lucky Button:** The "I'm Feeling Lucky" button's impact on advertising revenue highlights Google's commitment to providing users with efficient and relevant search results, even at the expense of potential profits.

6. **Acquisition Spree:** Google's extensive acquisition history reflects its strategy of expanding into new markets and technologies, diversifying its offerings beyond its core search engine product.

7. **Googleplex Campus:** The amenities at the Googleplex Campus illustrate the company's commitment to fostering a supportive and engaging work environment, which has become a model for other tech companies.

8. **Google's Impact on Language:** The inclusion of "to google" in the dictionary reflects Google's profound influence on modern language and culture, solidifying its status as a ubiquitous tool and verb.

9. **Environmental Initiatives:** Google's investments in renewable energy underscore its commitment to sustainability and corporate responsibility, setting a

precedent for tech companies to prioritize environmental stewardship.

10. **Moonshot Projects:** Alphabet's pursuit of moonshot projects emphasizes its ambition to tackle complex global challenges through innovation and technology, pushing the boundaries of what's possible.

11. **Market Dominance:** Google's dominance in the search engine market highlights its unparalleled reach and influence, shaping the digital landscape and influencing user behavior worldwide.

12. **Google's Birthday:** Celebrating Google's birthday on September 27th serves as a reminder of the company's humble beginnings and rapid growth into a global powerhouse in just a few decades.**Diverse Workforce:** Google's efforts to promote diversity and inclusion reflect its recognition of the value of diverse perspectives in driving innovation and addressing complex problems in the tech industry.

13. **Ad Revenue:** The significant revenue generated from advertising underscores Google's business model and its reliance on targeted advertising as a primary source of income.

14. **Global Reach:** Google's presence in over 100 languages and countries highlights its role as a truly global platform for accessing information and connecting people across borders and cultures.

15. **Privacy Concerns:** Scrutiny over privacy practices underscores the importance of protecting user data and maintaining trust in an era of increasing digital surveillance and data breaches.

16. **Philanthropic Efforts:** Google's philanthropic initiatives demonstrate its commitment to using its resources and expertise to address pressing social and environmental issues, contributing to positive change beyond its core business.

17. **Alphabet Restructure:** Google's reorganization under Alphabet reflects its strategic evolution and allows for greater focus and autonomy in pursuing diverse ventures and moonshot projects.

18. **AI Research:** Google's leadership in AI research highlights its role in shaping the future of technology and its potential to revolutionize industries ranging from healthcare to transportation.

19. **Cultural Icon:** Google's status as a cultural icon underscores its profound impact on society and its role as a

symbol of innovation, accessibility, and the democratization of information.

1

Embrace the Habit of Daily Inquiry

The Transformative Power of Lifelong Learning

Introduction to Daily Inquiry:

In Chapter 1 of "Google Something Every Day," we explore the profound impact of making learning a daily habit. By committing to the simple yet powerful act of Googling something new each day, individuals can cultivate a mindset of curiosity and inquiry that keeps their minds sharp and engaged. In this section, we will discuss practical strategies for incorporating daily inquiry into one's routine and the transformative benefits it can bring.

Understanding the Power of Daily Inquiry:

At its core, daily inquiry is about embracing a mindset of curiosity and lifelong learning. It's about recognizing that every day presents an opportunity to expand our knowledge, challenge our assumptions, and explore new ideas. By making a conscious effort to seek out new information and perspectives, we can keep our minds flexible and adaptable, ready to tackle whatever challenges come our way.

Practical Strategies for Daily Inquiry:

Incorporating daily inquiry into one's routine doesn't have to be complicated. Here are some practical strategies for making learning a daily habit:

1. **Start Small:** Begin by setting aside just a few minutes each day for inquiry. Whether it's during your morning coffee break or before bed, find a time that works for you and commit to it.

2. **Keep a Curiosity Journal:** Start a journal where you can jot down questions, ideas, and interesting topics to explore further. Use this journal as a guide for your daily inquiries.

3. **Set Goals:** Challenge yourself to learn something new each day. Set specific goals for what you want to learn or accomplish, whether it's mastering a new skill, understanding a complex concept, or exploring a new

hobby.

4. **Use Technology to Your Advantage:** Leverage the power of the internet and search engines like Google to access a wealth of information on any topic imaginable. Take advantage of online courses, tutorials, and resources to deepen your understanding and expand your horizons. How do you find them? Google em."

The Transformative Benefits of Daily Inquiry:

The act of daily inquiry offers a wide range of transformative benefits, including:

1. **Increased Knowledge and Understanding:** By actively seeking out new information and perspectives, individuals can expand their knowledge base and deepen their understanding of the world around them.

2. **Improved Critical Thinking Skills:** Daily inquiry encourages individuals to question assumptions, challenge conventional wisdom, and think critically about the information they encounter. This, in turn, enhances problem-solving abilities and decision-making skills.

3. **Enhanced Creativity and Innovation:** Regular exposure to new ideas and perspectives stimulates creativity and fosters innovation. By exploring diverse topics and making

unexpected connections, individuals can unleash their creative potential and generate fresh insights and ideas.

4. **Greater Resilience and Adaptability:** Cultivating a mindset of curiosity and inquiry helps individuals develop greater resilience and adaptability in the face of change and uncertainty. By embracing lifelong learning, individuals can navigate challenges more effectively and thrive in an ever-evolving world.

Conclusion:

Embracing the habit of daily inquiry is a powerful tool for personal growth and development. By committing to Googling something new each day, individuals can cultivate a mindset of curiosity and lifelong learning that keeps their minds sharp, engaged, and ready to tackle whatever challenges come their way. So, let's embrace the transformative power of daily inquiry and unlock endless opportunities for growth, discovery, and innovation.

2

Cultivate a Curious Mindset

Unleashing the Power of Lifelong Learning

Understanding the Importance of Curiosity

Curiosity is often described as the engine of learning and innovation. It's the innate desire to explore, discover, and understand the world around us. In Chapter 2 of "Google Something Every Day," we delve into the transformative power of cultivating a curious mindset. By nurturing our natural sense of wonder and embracing a mindset of lifelong learning, we can unlock new insights, deepen our understanding, and fuel our passion for discovery.

Embracing Lifelong Learning

At its core, cultivating a curious mindset is about embracing the idea that learning is a lifelong journey. It's about recognizing that there's always something new to discover, no matter how much we already know. By approaching each day with a sense of wonder and curiosity, we open ourselves up to endless opportunities for growth and exploration.

Practical Strategies for Cultivating Curiosity

Cultivating a curious mindset doesn't happen overnight. It requires intentional effort and practice. Here are some practical strategies for nurturing curiosity in our daily lives:

1. **Ask Questions:** Curiosity begins with asking questions. Encourage yourself to question assumptions, challenge conventional wisdom, and seek out new information. Don't be afraid to ask "why" or "how" when faced with something you don't understand.

2. **Explore Diverse Topics:** Variety is the spice of life, and the same holds true for curiosity. Try to explore a wide range of topics and disciplines, from science and history to art and literature. Expose yourself to new ideas, perspectives, and experiences to keep your curiosity alive and thriving.

3. **Stay Open-Minded:** Cultivating a curious mindset requires an open-minded approach to learning. Be willing to consider new ideas, even if they challenge your existing beliefs or viewpoints. Approach each new experience with a sense of openness and curiosity, and you'll be amazed at what you can discover.

The Transformative Benefits of Curiosity

The benefits of cultivating a curious mindset are far-reaching and transformative. Here are just a few of the ways curiosity can enhance our lives:

1. **Enhanced Learning and Understanding:** Curiosity fuels a desire to learn and understand the world around us. By approaching new experiences with a curious mindset, we can deepen our understanding of complex concepts and discover new insights and perspectives.

2. **Increased Creativity and Innovation:** Curiosity stimulates creativity and fosters innovation. By exploring diverse topics and making unexpected connections, we can unleash our creative potential and generate fresh ideas and solutions.

3. **Greater Resilience and Adaptability:** Curiosity encourages a willingness to explore and experiment, even in the face of uncertainty. This resilience and adaptability

are essential traits for navigating life's challenges and thriving in an ever-changing world.

Conclusion

Cultivating a curious mindset is a powerful tool for personal growth and development. By embracing lifelong learning and approaching each day with a sense of wonder and curiosity, we can unlock new opportunities for growth, discovery, and innovation. So, let's embrace the transformative power of curiosity and embark on a journey of lifelong learning and exploration.

3

Expand Your Knowledge Base

Embracing Lifelong Learning Across Diverse Disciplines

Introduction to Expanding Your Knowledge Base

In Chapter 3 of "Google Something Every Day," we delve into the transformative power of expanding our knowledge base through lifelong learning. Learning is not confined to a classroom or a specific stage of life; it is a continuous journey with no end in sight. By exploring a diverse range of topics and disciplines, we open ourselves up to new ideas, perspectives, and opportunities for growth.

Embracing Lifelong Learning

At its core, expanding our knowledge base is about embracing the idea that learning is a lifelong journey. It's about recognizing that there's always something new to discover, no matter how much we already know. By approaching each day with a sense of curiosity and openness, we can unlock new insights, deepen our understanding, and enrich our lives in countless ways.

Practical Strategies for Expanding Your Knowledge Base

Expanding your knowledge base requires intentional effort and a willingness to explore new ideas and perspectives. Here are some practical strategies for incorporating lifelong learning into your daily routine:

1. **Pursue Your Passions:** Start by exploring topics that genuinely interest you. Whether it's science, history, art, or technology, follow your curiosity and delve into subjects that ignite your passion.

2. **Read Widely:** Reading is one of the most effective ways to expand your knowledge base. Try to read books, articles, and essays across a variety of genres and disciplines. Don't limit yourself to one subject; instead, embrace diversity in your reading habits.

3. **Take Online Courses:** In today's digital age, there are countless opportunities for learning online. Explore platforms like Coursera, Udemy, and Khan Academy to find courses on topics that interest you. Whether you want to learn a new language, master a skill, or explore a new subject, online courses offer a convenient and flexible way to expand your knowledge base.

4. **Attend Workshops and Seminars:** Look for workshops, seminars, and conferences in your area that cover topics you're interested in. These events provide valuable opportunities to gain experience from experts in the field, connect with like-minded individuals, and expand your network.

The Transformative Benefits of Expanding Your Knowledge Base

Expanding your knowledge base offers a wide range of transformative benefits, including:

Enhanced Problem-Solving Skills: By exposing yourself to diverse perspectives and ideas, you develop the ability to approach problems from multiple angles and find innovative solutions.

Increased Creativity and Innovation: Learning across diverse disciplines stimulates creativity and fosters innovation. By making unexpected connections between seemingly unrelated topics, you can generate fresh ideas and insights.

Greater Empathy and Understanding: Learning about different cultures, histories, and viewpoints fosters empathy and understanding. It helps you appreciate the diversity of human experiences and build stronger connections with others.

Improved Decision-Making Abilities: Expanding your knowledge base equips you with the information and insights needed to make informed decisions in all areas of your life. Whether it's choosing a career path, making financial decisions, or navigating complex social issues, a broad knowledge base enhances your decision-making abilities.

Conclusion

Expanding your knowledge base is a lifelong journey that offers endless opportunities for growth and discovery. By embracing lifelong learning and exploring a diverse range of topics and disciplines, you can deepen your understanding of the world, enhance your problem-solving skills, and enrich your life in countless ways. So, let's embrace the transformative power of expanding our knowledge base and embark on a journey of lifelong learning and exploration.

4

Apply What You Learn

Turning Knowledge into Action for Personal Growth and Success

Introduction to Applying What You Learn

In Chapter 4 of "Google Something Every Day," we explore the critical importance of applying what we learn in our daily lives. While acquiring knowledge is essential, it's only through practical application that we truly internalize and benefit from what we've learned. Whether it's solving problems, pursuing new interests, or sharing our knowledge with others, the act of applying what we learn helps solidify our understanding and reinforces our learning.

The Value of Practical Application

Knowledge is only valuable when it's put into practice. In this section, we delve into the transformative benefits of applying what we learn:

1. **Reinforces Learning:** Applying what we learn helps reinforce our understanding of the material. By putting concepts into action, we engage with the material on a deeper level and internalize it more effectively.

2. **Builds Confidence:** Taking action based on what we've learned builds confidence in our abilities. As we see the positive results of our efforts, we become more confident in our knowledge and skills.

3. **Sparks Creativity:** Applying what we learn often requires creative problem-solving. By engaging with real-world challenges, we are forced to think creatively and come up with innovative solutions.

Practical Strategies for Applying What You Learn

Here are some practical strategies for applying what you learn in your daily life:

1. **Set Clear Goals:** Before applying what you have learned, it's essential to have clear goals in mind. Define what you

want to achieve and how you plan to do it.

2.   **Break It Down:** Break down your goals into smaller, manageable tasks. This makes them more achievable and helps you stay focused and motivated.

3.   **Take Action:** Don't wait for the perfect moment to start applying what you have learned. Take action now, even if it's just a small step in the right direction.

4.   **Reflect and Adjust:** As you apply what you have learned, take time to reflect on your progress. Evaluate what is working well and what could be improved, then adjust your approach accordingly.

The Transformative Benefits of Applying What You Learn

Applying what you learn offers numerous transformative benefits, including:

1.   **Skill Development:** By putting your knowledge into practice, you develop valuable skills that are essential for personal and professional success.

2.   **Problem-Solving Abilities:** Practical application hones your problem-solving abilities and equips you with the tools needed to overcome challenges in all areas of life.

3. **Enhanced Creativity:** Engaging with real-world problems stimulates creativity and encourages innovative thinking.

4. **Increased Confidence:** Successfully applying what you have learned boosts your confidence and self-esteem, empowering you to take on new challenges with courage and conviction.

Conclusion

Applying what you learn is essential for personal growth, success, and fulfillment. By putting your knowledge into action, you reinforce your learning, develop valuable skills, and build confidence in your abilities. So, let's embrace the transformative power of applying what we learn and take proactive steps to turn knowledge into action in our daily lives.

5

Foster a Community of Learners

The Power of Connection and Collaboration in Lifelong Learning

Introduction to Fostering a Community of Learners

In Chapter 5 of "Google Something Every Day," we delve into the transformative power of fostering a community of learners. Learning is not a solitary endeavor; it thrives in a supportive community where individuals can connect, collaborate, and grow together. By joining online forums, attending meetups, and engaging with like-minded individuals, we can create a community of learners that inspires, motivates, and supports us on our journey of continuous growth.

The Importance of Community in Learning

Learning is inherently social. We learn from one another through shared experiences, insights, and perspectives. In this section, w explore the critical importance of community in learning:

1. **Inspiration and Motivation:** Being part of a community of learners provides inspiration and motivation to pursue our goals. Seeing others succeed and overcome challenges encourages us to push ourselves further and strive for excellence.

2. **Collaboration and Support:** A supportive community provides a safe space for collaboration and sharing. Whether it's seeking advice, exchanging ideas, or offering support, community members can lean on one another for guidance and encouragement.

3. **Accountability:** Being part of a community holds us accountable for our learning goals. Knowing that others are cheering us on and expecting us to succeed motivates us to stay committed and focused on our objectives.

Practical Strategies for Fostering a Community of Learners

Here are some practical strategies for fostering a community of learners:

1. **Join Online Forums and Communities:** Explore online forums, social media groups, and online learning platforms to connect with like-minded individuals who share your passion for learning. Participate in discussions, ask questions, and share your own insights and experiences.

2. **Attend Meetups and Workshops:** Look for local meetups, workshops, and events related to your areas of interest. These gatherings provide valuable opportunities to meet new people, network with professionals, and engage in collaborative learning activities.

3. **Start a Study Group:** Form a study group with friends, colleagues, or classmates to support one another in your learning endeavors. Meet regularly to discuss course material, share resources, and work on projects together.

4. **Volunteer or Mentor:** Give back to your community by volunteering your time and expertise to mentor others. Whether it's tutoring students, leading workshops, or participating in community outreach programs, mentoring is a rewarding way to share your knowledge and skills with others.

The Transformative Benefits of Fostering a Community of Learners

Fostering a community of learners offers numerous transformative benefits, including:

1. **Expanded Networks:** Connecting with like-minded individuals expands your professional and social networks, opening up new opportunities for collaboration, mentorship, and personal growth.

2. **Shared Learning Experiences:** Engaging with others in a community of learners provides opportunities for shared learning experiences, where members can learn from one another's successes, failures, and insights.

3. **Increased Motivation and Accountability:** Being part of a supportive community boosts motivation and holds members accountable for their learning goals. Knowing that others are rooting for you and expecting you to succeed encourages you to stay focused and committed to your objectives.

4. **Enhanced Creativity and Innovation:** Collaborating with others in a community of learners stimulates creativity and fosters innovation. By exchanging ideas, exploring new perspectives, and working together on projects, members can generate fresh insights and solutions to

complex problems.

Conclusion

Fostering a community of learners is a powerful way to enhance your learning experience and accelerate your personal and professional growth. By connecting with like-minded individuals, sharing resources, and collaborating on projects, you can create a supportive network that inspires, motivates, and supports you on your journey of continuous learning. So, let's embrace the transformative power of community and work together to create a brighter future for ourselves and others.

6

Make a Positive Impact

Using Knowledge and Skills to Serve Others and Build a Better World

Introduction to Making a Positive Impact

Chapter 6 of "Google Something Every Day" focuses on the profound importance of making a positive impact on the world around us. Just as Admiral McRaven emphasized the significance of leaving a positive mark, we too can contribute to the betterment of society by sharing our knowledge and experiences with others. Whether through volunteering, mentoring, or teaching, we have the power to make a meaningful difference in the lives of those around us.

Understanding the Importance of Making a Positive Impact

Making a positive impact is about more than just personal fulfillment; it's about creating a ripple effect of positive change that extends far beyond ourselves. In this section, we explore the significance of making a positive impact:

1. **Building Stronger Communities:** Making a positive impact strengthens communities by fostering connections, promoting collaboration, and empowering individuals to reach their full potential.

2. **Creating a Legacy of Service:** Making a positive impact leaves a lasting legacy of service and goodwill that continues to inspire and uplift future generations.

3. **Fostering Personal Growth:** Making a positive impact challenges us to step outside of our comfort zones, develop new skills, and grow as individuals. It enriches our lives and deepens our sense of purpose and fulfillment.

Practical Strategies for Making a Positive Impact

Here are some practical strategies for making a positive impact in your community:

1. **Volunteer Your Time:** Look for opportunities to volunteer with local organizations and charities that align with your interests and values. Whether it's serving meals at a soup kitchen, tutoring students, or cleaning up a local park, volunteering is a powerful way to give back to your community and make a tangible difference in the lives of others.

2. **Mentorship and Coaching:** Share your knowledge and expertise with others by becoming a mentor or coach. Whether it's mentoring a young professional in your field or coaching a youth sports team, mentorship provides invaluable support and guidance to individuals striving to achieve their goals.

3. **Teach and Educate:** Use your knowledge and skills to educate others by teaching classes, leading workshops, or hosting informational sessions. Whether it's teaching a cooking class, leading a financial literacy workshop, or sharing your expertise in a particular subject area, teaching provides an opportunity to empower others through knowledge and education.

The Transformative Benefits of Making a Positive Impact

Making a positive impact offers numerous transformative benefits, including:

1. **Sense of Purpose and Fulfillment:** Making a positive impact gives us a sense of purpose and fulfillment by allowing us to contribute to something greater than ourselves.

2. **Strengthened Relationships:** Making a positive impact strengthens our relationships with others by fostering trust, collaboration, and mutual respect.

3. **Personal Growth and Development:** Making a positive impact challenges us to grow and develop as individuals by pushing us out of our comfort zones and expanding our skills and abilities.

Conclusion

Making a positive impact is a powerful way to use our knowledge and skills to serve others and build a better world. Whether through volunteering, mentoring, or teaching, we have the opportunity to make a meaningful difference in the lives of those around us and leave a lasting legacy of service and goodwill. So, let's embrace the transformative power of making a positive impact and work together to create a brighter future for ourselves and others.

7

Others Besides Google

There Are Other Search Engines Besides Google

After you Become Proficient Using Google, Try Other Search Engines

To this point we have been talking about and suggesting that you "Google Something Every Day" but there are other search engines in addition to Google. Let's dive deeper into the others, their types, differences, and uses of some other search engines besides Google:

1. **Bing:**

   - **Type:** Bing is a general-purpose search engine developed by Microsoft.

- **Differences:** Bing's search results may differ from Google's due to variations in algorithms and indexing methods. It also integrates with Microsoft services such as Outlook, Office, and Xbox.

- **Uses:** Bing is commonly used for web searches, but it also powers search on various Microsoft products and services. It offers features like Bing Maps, Bing News, and Bing Ads.

2. **Yahoo:**

- **Type:** Yahoo Search is a search engine owned by Verizon Media.

- **Differences:** Yahoo Search's results are powered by Bing's index as part of a partnership between Yahoo and Microsoft. It provides a portal-like experience with news, email, and other services alongside search functionality.

- **Uses:** Yahoo Search is often used for general web searches, accessing news, checking email (via Yahoo Mail), and browsing Yahoo's other content offerings.

3. DuckDuckGo:

- **Type:** DuckDuckGo is a privacy-focused search engine.

- **Differences:** DuckDuckGo does not track user data or personalize search results. It sources its search results from various sources, including its own web crawler, Bing, Yahoo, and others.

- **Uses:** DuckDuckGo is popular among users concerned about privacy and tracking. It is used for general web searches, especially by those who prefer not to have their search history recorded.

4. Baidu:

- **Type:** Baidu is the leading search engine in China.

- **Differences**: Baidu's search results are tailored for the Chinese language and culture. It offers a wide range of services beyond search, including maps, news, online encyclopedia, and cloud storage.

- **Uses:** Baidu is the go-to search engine for users in China, used for web searches, maps, news, and various online services.

5. Yandex:

- **Type:** Yandex is the dominant search engine in Russia.

- **Differences:** Yandex's search algorithms are optimized for the Russian language and its nuances. It offers a suite of services including search, maps, translation, and cloud storage.

- **Uses:** Yandex is widely used in Russia for web searches, maps, translations, and accessing various online services provided by Yandex.

6. Ask.com:

- **Type:** Ask.com is a question-and-answer search engine.

- **Differences:** Ask.com allows users to ask questions in their natural language and provides search results based on those queries. It also offers curated content and answers from experts.

- **Uses:** Ask.com is used for finding specific answers to questions, accessing expert advice, and discovering curated content on assorted topics.

These search engines cater to diverse user needs, ranging from general web searches to specialized services, and they differ in terms of their focus, algorithms, user interfaces, and additional features.

YAHOO!

DuckDuckGo

Yandex

8

Uses, Instructions, and Practice

How Can You Use These
Other Search Engines

Let's Actually Try Them.

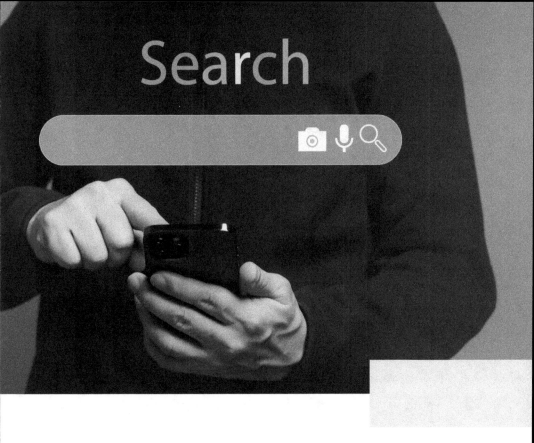

Here are some actual examples of how you can use each of these search engines along with instructions on how to practice these uses:

1. Bing:

Use: Web searches, finding locations, accessing news.

Instructions:

- Go to Bing.com in your web browser.

- In the search bar, type your query (e.g., "best restaurants near me").

- Press Enter or click on the magnifying glass icon to perform the search.

- Explore the search results, including web links, images, videos, news articles, and maps.

2. Yahoo:

Use: Web searches, checking email, accessing news.

Instructions:

- Visit Yahoo.com in your web browser.

- If you want to perform a web search, enter your query in the search bar at the top of the page and press Enter.

- To access news or other content, navigate to the respective sections on the Yahoo homepage.

- If you have a Yahoo email account, click on "Mail" at the top-right corner to sign in and check your email.

3. DuckDuckGo:

Use: Private web searches, avoiding personalized results.

Instructions:

- Go to www.DuckDuckGo.com in your web browser.

- Enter your search query in the search bar and press Enter.

- DuckDuckGo will provide search results without tracking your activity or personalizing the results based on your past searches.

4. Baidu:

Use: Web searches, maps, news, accessing online services in China.

Instructions:

- Visit www.Baidu.com in your web browser (Note: Baidu's interface may be primarily in Chinese).

- Enter your search query in the search bar and press Enter.

- Explore the search results, including web links, maps, news articles, and other services offered by Baidu.

5. Yandex:

Use: Web searches, maps, translations, accessing online services in Russia.

Instructions:

- Go to www.Yandex.ru in your web browser.

- Enter your search query in the search bar and press Enter.

- Yandex will provide search results tailored for the Russian language and culture, along with access to maps, translation services, and other features.

6. Ask.com:

Use: Asking specific questions, accessing expert advice.

Instructions:

- Visit www.Ask.com in your web browser.

- Type your question in natural language in the search bar and press Enter.

- Ask.com will provide search results that aim to directly answer your question, along with curated content and expert advice related to your query.

9

Key Words

Key Words Are
the Foundation for
Productive Search
Engine, Searches.

What Are Key Words and How Do You Use Them?

Keywords play a fundamental role in the realm of Search Engine Optimization (SEO) and digital marketing. They are essentially the words or phrases that users type into search engines when looking for information, products, or services. Understanding keywords and how to use them effectively can significantly impact the visibility and success of online content on platforms like Google and other search engines.

Keywords serve as the bridge between what users are searching for and the content that websites provide. When a user enters a keyword into a search engine, the search engine's algorithm scours the web for relevant content that matches or relates to that keyword. Websites that have optimized their content with the right keywords are more likely to appear in the search results, increasing their visibility and attracting organic traffic.

There are several types of keywords that digital marketers and website owners focus on:

1. **Short-tail Keywords:** These are short and general keywords consisting of one or two words, such as "shoes" or "fitness." Short-tail keywords typically have high search volumes but are also highly competitive.

2. **Long-tail Keywords:** Long-tail keywords are longer and more specific phrases, usually containing three or more words, such as "best running shoes for flat feet" or "how to lose weight fast." Long-tail keywords have lower search volumes but are less competitive, making it easier to rank for them.

3. **Branded Keywords:** These are keywords that include the brand name of a company or product, such as "Nike shoes" or "Apple iPhone." Branded keywords are often used by users who are already familiar with a particular brand and are further along in the buyer's journey.

4. **Transactional Keywords:** Transactional keywords

indicate that the user is ready to make a purchase or take a specific action. Examples include "buy iPhone online" or "download free e-book."

5. **Informational Keywords:** Informational keywords are used when users are seeking information or answers to their questions. Examples include "how to tie a tie" or "benefits of meditation."

Now, let's discuss how to use keywords effectively to improve visibility on Google and other search engines:

1. **Keyword Research:** The first step is to conduct thorough keyword research to identify the most relevant and high-performing keywords for your content. Use keyword research tools like Google Keyword Planner, SEMrush, or Ahrefs to discover relevant keywords, analyze search volumes, and assess competition levels.

2. **Keyword Placement:** Once you have identified your target keywords, strategically place them throughout your content, including in titles, headings, meta descriptions, and body paragraphs. However, avoid overstuffing your content with keywords, as this can lead to keyword spamming and penalties from search engines.

3. **Content Optimization:** Create high-quality, informative content that aligns with the intent behind the chosen keywords. Ensure that your content provides value to users and answers their queries effectively. Use keywords naturally within the content without compromising readability or user experience.

4. **On-Page Optimization:** Optimize various on-page elements, such as URLs, image alt tags, and internal linking, to include relevant keywords and improve search engine visibility. This helps search engines understand the context and relevance of your content.

5. **Monitor and Adjust:** Continuously monitor the performance of your keywords and content using analytics tools like Google Analytics or Search Console. Track rankings, organic traffic, and user engagement metrics to identify areas for improvement and make adjustments accordingly.

6. **Stay Updated:** Stay informed about changes in search engine algorithms and trends in user behavior to adapt your keyword strategy accordingly. Search engine algorithms are constantly evolving, so it is essential to stay updated to maintain and improve your search engine rankings.

In summary, keywords are essential components of SEO and digital

marketing strategies, serving as the foundation for improving visibility and attracting organic traffic from search engines like Google. By conducting thorough keyword research, strategically incorporating keywords into content, and continuously monitoring performance, website owners and digital marketers can optimize their online presence and reach their target audience effectively.

10

The Holy Grail of Keyword Search Examples

Applying What You Have Learned.

The Opportunities in Searching Keywords as Your Reward for Learning.

Here is the chapter you may have been waiting for. Or maybe it's the one you found first if you know a little about the subject and started this book at the end.

It's the "The light at the end of the tunnel." -- It's the "Pot at the end of the rainbow." -- It's the "Holy Grail" of reward for those who reaped. It's where you can copy and enter some pretty cool keywords into Google or the search engine of your choice and actually see some results for your information, entertainment, and education.

Simply follow the 10 sets of instructions below. Enter the suggested keywords into Google (Or a search engine of your choice) to open the door to the pandora's box or results. But "Don't Stop" at the suggested websites. When you see what opens as a result of your search, do what I did in 1983 when I was first introduced to the marvel and miracle of the personal computer. Ask yourself, "If it did 'that' and found 'that' information, what if I entered, 'this'…?"

I.   Below are 10 keywords you can enter into Google to search to find OLD-TIME WESTERN MOVIES:

1. **Classic Western Movies** This search will return results for iconic western films from the golden age of Hollywood, featuring legendary actors, classic storylines, and memorable settings in the American West.

2. **Vintage Cowboy Films** These are old films depicting the cowboy lifestyle, often shot in black and white or early color, capturing the essence of the Wild West era with themes of adventure, justice, and rugged individualism.

3. **Old-Time Westerns** This search will yield results for early western films produced during the heyday of the genre, typically characterized by simple plots, straightforward morality, and action-packed showdowns.

4. **Golden Age Western Movies** These are films from the peak period of western cinema, usually referring to

the 1940s to the 1960s, featuring influential directors, celebrated actors, and classic narratives that have stood the test of time.

5. **Retro Cowboy Films** These films evoke a nostalgic feel, often produced in later decades but inspired by the style and themes of classic westerns, with a focus on authenticity and homage to the genre's roots.

6. **Traditional Western Movies** These films adhere closely to the conventions and tropes established by early westerns, including cowboys, outlaws, saloons, and wide-open landscapes, offering a timeless portrayal of the American frontier.

7. **Vintage Westerns** Similar to "classic western movies," this search will return results for older western films that have retained their appeal and cultural significance over time, appealing to fans of vintage cinema and western enthusiasts alike.

8. **Old-Fashioned Cowboy Movies** These films harken back to a simpler era of filmmaking, featuring traditional cowboy heroes, daring adventures, and moral conflicts set against the backdrop of the untamed West.

9. **Classic Wild West Films** This search will bring up films that capture the essence of the Wild West period,

depicting the rugged landscape, lawlessness, and larger-than-life characters that defined this iconic era in American history.

10. **Golden Era Western Movies** Similar to "golden age western movies," this search will return results for films produced during the peak period of western cinema, known for their high production values, compelling storytelling, and enduring popularity among audiences.

II. **Below are 10 general websites (not keywords) where you might find HIGHLIGHTS OF WORLD SERIES GAMES:**

1. **MLB.com** The official website of Major League Baseball (MLB), providing news, scores, statistics, schedules, and information about teams, players, and events in professional baseball.

2. **ESPN.com** The website of ESPN, a leading sports network, offers coverage of various sports leagues and events, including news articles, analysis, highlights, scores, and streaming content.

3. **YouTube.com** A popular video-sharing platform where users can watch, upload, and share videos on a wide range of topics, including sports highlights, interviews, analysis, and fan-generated content related

to baseball and other sports.

4. **FoxSports.com** The website of Fox Sports, a sports media network, featuring news, analysis, scores, and highlights from various sports leagues, including Major League Baseball (MLB).

5. **MLB.TV** MLB's official streaming service, offering subscribers access to live and on-demand broadcasts of MLB games, including out-of-market games, along with additional features such as DVR functionality and multi-game viewing.

6. **NBCSports.com** The website of NBC Sports, providing coverage of sports leagues and events, including news, analysis, scores, and highlights from Major League Baseball (MLB) and other sports.

7. **CBS Sports** The sports division of CBS, offering coverage of various sports leagues and events, including news, analysis, scores, and highlights from Major League Baseball (MLB) and other sports.

8. **WatchESPN** ESPN's online streaming platform, offering live and on-demand access to ESPN's network of channels, including coverage of Major League Baseball (MLB) games, along with other sports programming.

9. **Hulu** A subscription-based streaming service offering a wide range of TV shows, movies, and original content, including sports-related programming and highlights, though the availability of specific sports content may vary.

10. **Reddit** A social news aggregation and discussion website where users can share and discuss content from around the web, including sports-related topics such as Major League Baseball (MLB), with dedicated communities (subreddits) for baseball fans to engage with each other.

III. **Below are 10 keywords you can enter into Google to search for NUTRITIONAL DIETS FOR SENIORS:**

1. **Elderly Nutrition** Information and resources on nutrition for older adults, including dietary recommendations, meal planning tips, and strategies to address age-related nutritional needs and challenges.

2. **Geriatric Diet** Guidance on nutrition specifically tailored to the needs of older adults, taking into account factors such as changes in metabolism, digestion, and nutrient absorption that occur with aging.

3. **Senior Nutrition** Resources and advice on maintaining a healthy diet as one ages, including tips

for managing chronic conditions, promoting optimal health, and addressing common nutritional concerns faced by seniors.

4. **Healthy Aging Diet** Information on dietary patterns and food choices that support healthy aging, including recommendations for nutrient-rich foods, portion control, and lifestyle factors that contribute to overall well-being in older adults.

5. **Nutritional Needs for Older Adults** Guidance on meeting the unique nutritional requirements of older adults, including adequate intake of protein, vitamins, minerals, and fiber to support healthy aging and prevent age-related health issues.

6. **Balanced Diet for Seniors** Tips and advice on achieving a balanced diet that provides essential nutrients while accommodating changes in appetite, taste, and digestion that may occur with age.

7. **Age-Related Dietary Guidelines** Recommendations and guidelines for nutrition and dietary intake tailored to older adults, based on factors such as age, gender, activity level, and health status.

8. **Meal Planning for The Elderly** Strategies and resources for planning nutritious meals and snacks

for older adults, including tips for grocery shopping, cooking, and meal preparation to support optimal health and well-being.

9. **Senior-Friendly Recipes** Specifically designed with the nutritional needs and preferences of older adults in mind, featuring easy-to-prepare dishes that are flavorful, nutrient-dense, and suitable for various dietary restrictions.

10. **Nutritional Supplements for Older Adults** Information on dietary supplements commonly used by older adults to address specific nutritional deficiencies or health concerns, including vitamins, minerals, and other dietary supplements recommended for older adults.

IV. **Below are 10 keywords you can enter into Google to search for OLD-TIME TV SHOWS**

1. **Westerns** Results related to the genre of Western films and television shows, featuring cowboys, outlaws, frontier towns, and iconic landscapes of the American West, with themes of adventure, justice, and rugged individualism.

2. **Sitcoms** Content related to situational comedies, a genre of television programming featuring recurring

characters in humorous situations, typically set in everyday settings such as homes, workplaces, or social gatherings.

3. **Detective Series** Information and resources about television series featuring detectives or investigators solving crimes or mysteries, often in a procedural format, with elements of suspense, investigation, and crime-solving.

4. **Sci-Fi** Results related to science fiction, a genre of speculative fiction exploring futuristic or imaginative concepts such as space travel, advanced technology, extraterrestrial life, and alternate realities, often set in the future or outer space.

5. **Family Dramas** Content focused on television dramas centered around families and interpersonal relationships, exploring themes such as love, loss, conflict, and resilience within familial dynamics.

6. **Variety Shows** Information about television programs featuring a mix of musical performances, comedy sketches, celebrity interviews, and other entertainment segments, offering a diverse and eclectic mix of content within a single show.

7. **Game Shows** Content related to television programs in which contestants compete in various challenges or trivia games to win prizes or cash rewards, often featuring interactive elements and audience participation.

8. **Adventure Series** Results related to television series featuring characters embarking on thrilling journeys or quests, often set in exotic locations or historical periods, with elements of action, exploration, and suspense.

9. **Medical Dramas** Information and resources about television dramas set in hospitals or medical settings, focusing on the lives and work of healthcare professionals, patient cases, ethical dilemmas, and personal struggles.

10. **Historical Dramas** Content focused on television dramas set in the past, exploring historical events, figures, or time periods, with an emphasis on authenticity, period detail, and storytelling within a historical context.

V. **Below are 10 keywords you can enter into Google to search for information related to ELVIS PRESLEY:** (Here is a mind-blowing example of "If it found 'that', what else can it find?" Simply change the name Elvis Presley to any other name you would like. I.e., George Washington. Bing Crosby. Buddy Holly. Bill Clinton. Arnold Palmer. Get the idea? You can search for anyone, or basically anything.) Just type it into Google and see what it finds.

1. **Elvis Presley Biography** Information and resources about the life story of Elvis Presley, including details about his upbringing, rise to fame, personal relationships, career milestones, and legacy as a cultural icon.

2. **Elvis Presley Music** Content related to the musical career of Elvis Presley, including his iconic songs, albums, performances, and contributions to various genres such as rock and roll, gospel, blues, and country music.

3. **Elvis Presley Movies** Information about the films in which Elvis Presley starred as an actor, including plot summaries, cast members, critical reception, and cultural impact of his work in the film industry.

4. **Elvis Presley Albums** Resources and details about the albums released by Elvis Presley throughout his career, including track listings, album covers, production credits, and commercial success of his music recordings.

5. **Elvis Presley Songs** Content related to individual songs recorded by Elvis Presley, including lyrics, music videos, live performances, and cultural significance of

his most popular and enduring musical compositions.

6. **Elvis Presley Discography** A comprehensive list of all the recordings made by Elvis Presley, including studio albums, live albums, compilation albums, and singles released over the course of his musical career.

7. **Elvis Presley Life** Further exploration of Elvis Presley's personal life beyond his public persona, including anecdotes, personal struggles, achievements, and insights into his character and personality.

8. **Elvis Presley Legacy** Discussion and analysis of the lasting impact and influence of Elvis Presley on music, entertainment, and popular culture, including tributes, honors, and ongoing appreciation of his work by fans and fellow artists.

9. **Elvis Presley Estate** Information about Graceland, the estate and mansion owned by Elvis Presley, including its history, tours, exhibits, and management by the Elvis Presley estate and preservation of his legacy.

10. **Elvis Presley Graceland** Specific details and resources about Graceland, including its architecture, interior design, artifacts, memorabilia, and visitor experience at the iconic home of Elvis Presley in Memphis, Tennessee.

VI. **Below are 10 keywords you can enter into Google to search for information on COMMON TYPES OF SURGERIES:**

1. **Appendectomy** Information about the surgical procedure to remove the appendix, typically performed to treat appendicitis, including details about the surgery process, recovery period, risks, and potential complications.

2. **Cataract Surgery** Resources and details about the surgical procedure to remove cataracts from the eye and replace them with artificial lenses, including information about pre-operative assessments, surgical techniques, and post-operative care.

3. **Knee Replacement Surgery** Information about the surgical procedure to replace a damaged or diseased knee joint with an artificial implant, including details about candidacy, surgical techniques, rehabilitation, and outcomes.

4. **Gallbladder Removal** (cholecystectomy) Details about the surgical procedure to remove the gallbladder, often performed to treat gallstones or gallbladder inflammation, including information about laparoscopic and open surgical techniques, recovery, and potential complications.

5. **Hysterectomy** Information about the surgical procedure to remove the uterus, either partially or completely, including details about the different types of hysterectomy, indications, surgical techniques, recovery, and potential effects on reproductive and overall health.

6. **Coronary Artery Bypass Surgery** Resources and details about the surgical procedure to restore blood flow to the heart by bypassing blocked or narrowed coronary arteries, including information about the surgical techniques, risks, recovery, and lifestyle changes post-surgery.

7. **Cesarean Section** (C-section) Information about the surgical procedure to deliver a baby through incisions made in the abdomen and uterus, including details about when and why it is performed, the procedure process, recovery, and potential risks and complications.

8. **Hernia Repair Surgery** Details about the surgical procedure to repair a hernia, including inguinal, umbilical, and hiatal hernias, including information about different surgical techniques, recovery, and potential risks and complications.

9. **Hip Replacement Surgery** Information about the surgical procedure to replace a damaged or diseased hip

joint with an artificial implant, including details about candidacy, surgical techniques, rehabilitation, and outcomes.

10. **Tonsillectomy** Resources and details about the surgical procedure to remove the tonsils, often performed to treat recurrent tonsillitis or breathing difficulties, including information about the procedure process, recovery, and potential risks and complications.

VII. **Below are 10 keywords you can enter into Google to search for information about WARS THE U.S.A. WAS INVLOVED IN:**

1. **American Revolutionary War** Information about the war fought between Great Britain and its Thirteen Colonies in North America from 1775 to 1783, resulting in the independence of the colonies and the formation of the United States of America.

2. **War of 1812** Resources and details about the conflict between the United States and Great Britain from 1812 to 1815, primarily over maritime issues such as trade restrictions and British impressment of American sailors, which ended in a stalemate.

3. **Mexican American War** Information about the war fought between the United States and Mexico from

1846 to 1848, resulting in the annexation of Texas and the acquisition of territory that would become California, Nevada, Utah, Arizona, New Mexico, Colorado, and Wyoming.

4. **American Civil War** Details about the devastating conflict fought between the Northern states (Union) and the Southern states (Confederacy) from 1861 to 1865, primarily over issues including slavery, states' rights, and federal authority, resulting in the abolition of slavery and the preservation of the Union.

5. **Spanish-American War** Resources and details about the brief conflict between the United States and Spain in 1898, resulting in the United States acquiring territories such as Puerto Rico, Guam, and the Philippines, and marking the emergence of the United States as a global power.

6. **World War I** Information about the global conflict fought from 1914 to 1918 between the Allies (including the United States, Great Britain, France, and Russia) and the Central Powers (including Germany, Austria-Hungary, and the Ottoman Empire), resulting in significant loss of life and redrawing of national boundaries.

7. **World War II** Details about the global conflict fought

from 1939 to 1945 involving the Allies (including the United States, Great Britain, Soviet Union, and China) and the Axis Powers (including Germany, Japan, and Italy), characterized by widespread warfare, genocide, and the emergence of the United States and the Soviet Union as superpowers.

8. **Korean War** Information about the conflict between North Korea (supported by China and the Soviet Union) and South Korea (supported by the United Nations, primarily the United States) from 1950 to 1953, resulting in a stalemate and the continued division of the Korean Peninsula.

9. **Vietnam War** Details about the conflict between North Vietnam (supported by the Soviet Union and China) and South Vietnam (supported by the United States and its allies), in which the user was involved as a member of the United States Army, from 1955 to 1975, resulting in the reunification of Vietnam under communist rule. (Shameless Plug: Your author, here, was in this one and wrote a book about it named "My Time Served in the United States Army,")

10. **Gulf War** Information about the military operation led by a coalition of nations, primarily the United States, against Iraq in 1990-1991, in response to its invasion of Kuwait, resulting in the liberation of Kuwait and

significant damage to Iraq's military infrastructure.

VIII. **Below are 10 keywords you can enter into Google to search for information on simple CAR PROBLEMS:**

1. **Car Won't Start** Information and resources on common reasons why a car may fail to start, including issues with the battery, starter motor, ignition switch, fuel system, or electrical connections, along with troubleshooting steps and potential solutions.

2. **Engine Misfire** Details about the symptoms, causes, and troubleshooting steps for an engine misfire, which may be due to issues such as faulty spark plugs, ignition coils, fuel injectors, or engine sensors, along with diagnostic techniques and repair procedures.

3. **Squeaky Brakes** Resources and information on why brakes may squeak when applied, including causes such as worn brake pads, brake dust buildup, rotor damage, or caliper issues, along with tips for diagnosis and repair to eliminate the noise.

4. **Dashboard Warning Lights** Explanation of common dashboard warning lights and their meanings, including indicators for issues such as engine problems, low tire pressure, battery issues, brake system faults, or malfunctioning vehicle systems, along with guidance

on what actions to take when these lights illuminate.

5. **Flat Tire** Information and resources on how to handle a flat tire situation, including steps for safely changing a tire, using a spare tire, and locating and repairing a puncture, along with tips for preventing flat tires and maintaining proper tire pressure.

6. **Burned-Out Headlights** Details about why headlights may burn out or dim over time, including causes such as worn-out bulbs, faulty wiring, or issues with the headlight assembly, along with guidance on how to replace headlight bulbs and troubleshoot headlight problems.

7. **Strange Noises While Driving** Explanation of common vehicle noises and their potential causes, including issues such as worn-out suspension components, engine belts, bearings, exhaust system problems, or transmission issues, along with diagnostic techniques and repair recommendations.

8. **Weak Air Conditioning** Information and resources on why an air conditioning system may blow warm or weak air, including causes such as low refrigerant levels, clogged air filters, compressor issues, or leaks in the system, along with troubleshooting steps and repair options.

9. **Faulty Battery Connection** Details about symptoms of a faulty battery connection, including issues such as difficulty starting the engine, dimming lights, or electrical malfunctions, along with guidance on how to check and clean battery terminals, tighten connections, and address battery-related problems.

10. **Worn-Out Windshield Wipers** Resources and information on signs of worn-out windshield wipers, including streaking, skipping, or poor wiping performance, along with guidance on how to inspect, replace, and maintain windshield wiper blades for optimal visibility and safety.

IX. **Below are 10 keywords you can enter into Google to search for information on PARTY GAMES:**

1. **Charades** A classic party game where players take turns acting out a word or phrase without speaking while their teammates try to guess what it is. It's a fun and interactive game that encourages creativity and teamwork.

2. **Pictionary** A drawing game where players take turns drawing a word or phrase on a piece of paper or whiteboard while their teammates try to guess what it is within a time limit. It's a lively and entertaining game that tests drawing skills and quick thinking.

3. **Trivia Pursuit** A trivia game where players answer questions from various categories such as history, science, entertainment, and sports to collect wedges and complete their game piece. It's a challenging and educational game that tests players' knowledge across a range of topics.

4. **Werewolf** A social deduction game where players are assigned roles as villagers or werewolves, with the villagers trying to identify and eliminate the werewolves before they are outnumbered. It's a strategic and suspenseful game that involves deception and deduction.

5. **Twister** A physical game where players place their hands and feet in colored circles on a large mat and try to maintain their balance while contorting their bodies to avoid falling over. It's a hilarious and energetic game that encourages flexibility and coordination.

6. **Cards Against Humanity** A party card game where players take turns playing cards with phrases or words to complete fill-in-the-blank statements, with often humorous or inappropriate results. It's a dark and irreverent game that sparks laughter and conversation.

7. **Mafia** A social deduction game similar to Werewolf where players are assigned roles as mafia members or civilians, with the mafia trying to eliminate civilians

without being caught, and civilians trying to identify and eliminate the mafia. It's a tense and engaging game that requires keen observation and persuasion skills.

8. **Minute to Win It** A series of quick and challenging one-minute games where players compete to complete tasks using everyday household items, such as stacking cups, balancing cookies, or moving objects with chopsticks. It's a fast-paced and exciting game that tests dexterity and quick thinking.

9. **Apples to Apples** A party card game where players take turns being the judge and selecting the best match for a given adjective from the cards played by the other players. It's a lighthearted and humorous game that encourages creativity and wit.

10. **Escape Room** A cooperative puzzle-solving game where players work together to solve a series of challenges and puzzles within a set time limit to "escape" from a themed room or scenario. It's an immersive and thrilling game that requires teamwork, communication, and problem-solving skills.

X. **Below are 10 keywords you can enter into Google to search for PLACES TO VISIT ON A BUDGET:**

1. **National Parks** Explore the natural beauty of National Parks, offering stunning landscapes, hiking trails, and opportunities for outdoor activities at a low entrance fee.

2. **Local Museums** Visit local museums, art galleries, and cultural centers, many of which offer free or discounted admission days, highlighting history, art, and culture.

3. **Beaches** Enjoy a day at the beach, soaking up the sun, swimming, and picnicking along the coastline, with many public beaches offering free access.

4. **Historic Sites** Discover historic landmarks, monuments, and heritage sites in your area, often offering free or low-cost tours and educational experiences.

5. **Botanical Gardens** Wander through botanical gardens and arboretums, highlighting a diverse array of plant species, landscapes, and seasonal displays, with many offering free admission.

6. **Local Parks** Spend time in local parks and green spaces, perfect for picnics, nature walks, and recreational activities such as cycling, jogging, or birdwatching.

7. **Street Markets** Explore vibrant street markets and flea markets, offering a variety of goods, foods, and cultural experiences, with opportunities for bargain hunting and sampling local cuisine.

8. **Historic Neighborhoods** Take a stroll through historic neighborhoods and districts, admiring architecture, street art, and local shops, often offering free walking tours or self-guided exploration.

9. **Library** Visit your local library, offering free access to books, magazines, movies, and educational resources, as well as community events, workshops, and activities.

10. **Scenic Drives** Embark on scenic drives through countryside, mountains, or coastal routes, offering breathtaking views and photo opportunities, with minimal cost for gas and vehicle maintenance.

I hope these exercises were enlightening and opened your mind to the endless opportunities that lie in being able to search on Google. As you become more familiar, you can broaden your searches by entering a sentence into Google, not just one or two words, for more detailed information about most anything. As an example, enter "How to make a kite."

Happy searching...

THANK YOU

I would like to extend my heartfelt gratitude to you for embarking on the transformative journey that has been outlined here within the pages of "Google Something Every Day."

Through the lens of my own life experiences and inspired by the timeless wisdom of Admiral McRaven's "Make Your Bed," I crafted this manifesto for lifelong learning that resonates with individuals of all ages and backgrounds. I sincerely hope you enjoyed it and reference it often.

By melding the principles of making your bed with the pursuit of knowledge, I tried to unveil a pathway to unlocking untapped potential and fostering positive change within oneself and the world. I hope I was successful.

Whether you're a seasoned technophile or a novice in the digital realm, I hope this book equipped you with the tools and mindset needed to embark on a journey of your own personal growth and discovery. If you agree, drop me a note.

Thank you for indulging me on this empowering journey of growth, fulfillment, and endless exploration. May the lessons learned within these pages guide you towards a future filled with purpose, joy, and the unwavering pursuit of knowledge.

Richard Erschik

Google

Credit to Google and Disclaimer:

We would like to extend our sincere appreciation to Google for their invaluable contribution to the world of information retrieval and knowledge dissemination. The use of the Google name and references to Google services throughout this book are intended solely for educational and illustrative purposes. Google is a registered trademark of Google LLC, and any mention of their services does not imply endorsement or affiliation with this book or its author.

Readers are encouraged to utilize Google's services responsibly and in accordance with Google's terms of service and privacy policy. The instructions provided in this book for using Google on various devices are intended to assist readers in accessing information effectively and efficiently. However, readers should exercise discretion and critical thinking when conducting online searches, and be mindful of the credibility and reliability of information obtained through internet sources.

Furthermore, the views and opinions expressed in this book are those of the author alone and do not necessarily reflect the views of Google LLC. Any similarities between the practices advocated in this book and those promoted by Google are purely coincidental.

ABOUT THE AUTHOR

Richard Erschik

Richard's unwavering dedication to lifelong learning and his commitment to empowering others through education have been the cornerstones of his remarkable journey. Throughout his career, Richard has undertaken numerous initiatives to enhance his own knowledge and skills while also sharing his expertise with others.

Richard's unwavering dedication to lifelong learning and his commitment to empowering others through education have been the cornerstones of his remarkable journey. Throughout his career, Richard has undertaken numerous initiatives to enhance his own knowledge and skills while also sharing his expertise with others. As a distinguished Army veteran, Richard's military service instilled in him a deep sense of discipline, resilience, and leadership. These qualities served as the foundation for his subsequent endeavors in the civilian world, where he continued to strive for excellence in every pursuit.

Richard's relentless pursuit of personal and professional growth led him to become an active member and award-winning speaker of Toastmasters International. By serving as the president of two active Toastmasters clubs simultaneously in South Florida, Richard not only honed his own speaking and leadership abilities but also mentored hundreds of individuals to overcome their fears and become confident communicators.

His contributions to the field of exhibitor education, recognized by prestigious industry associations and media publishers, further solidify his reputation as a thought leader and educator. Richard's engagements with renowned organizations such as ConExpo, the Society of Manufacturing Engineers, and the International Association of Exhibition Executives underscore his expertise in the areas of presentation skills, leadership development, and personal improvement.

Richard's insights and achievements have been featured in esteemed publications like the Chicago Tribune, Harvard Business Review, and Trade Show Executive magazine, where he has been listed as a Who's Who in exhibitor education. His willingness to share his knowledge and experiences with a broader audience reflects his genuine commitment to helping others succeed in their own endeavors.

In "Google Something Every Day," Richard leverages his extensive background in public speaking, leadership development, and personal improvement to provide readers with practical strategies for maximizing their use of Google as a tool for continuous learning and self-improvement. His credibility as a seasoned educator and communicator ensures that readers can trust in the value and authenticity of the insights shared in the book.

To learn more about Richard Erschik... "Google him!"

www.ingramcontent.com/pod-product-compliance
Lightning Source LLC
LaVergne TN
LVHW051709050326
832903LV00032B/4103